NEW ORLEANS
SAINTS
KENNY ABDO
Fly!
An Imprint of Abdo Zoom
abdobooks.com

abdobooks.com

Published by Abdo Zoom, a division of ABDO, P.O. Box 398166, Minneapolis, Minnesota 55439. Copyright © 2022 by Abdo Consulting Group, Inc. International copyrights reserved in all countries. No part of this book may be reproduced in any form without written permission from the publisher. Fly!™ is a trademark and logo of Abdo Zoom.

Printed in the United States of America, North Mankato, Minnesota.
052021
092021

Photo Credits: AP Images, Getty Images, iStock, Shutterstock PREMIER
Production Contributors: Kenny Abdo, Jennie Forsberg, Grace Hansen
Design Contributors: Candice Keimig, Neil Klinepier

Library of Congress Control Number: 2020919720

Publisher's Cataloging-in-Publication Data

Names: Abdo, Kenny, author.
Title: New Orleans Saints / by Kenny Abdo
Description: Minneapolis, Minnesota : Abdo Zoom, 2022 | Series: NFL teams |
    Includes online resources and index.
Identifiers: ISBN 9781098224738 (lib. bdg.) | ISBN 9781098225674 (ebook) |
    ISBN 9781098226145 (Read-to-Me ebook)
Subjects: LCSH: New Orleans Saints (Football team)--Juvenile literature. | National
    Football League--Juvenile literature. | Football teams--Juvenile literature. |
    American football--Juvenile literature. | Professional sports--Juvenile literature.
Classification: DDC 796.33264--dc23

TABLE OF CONTENTS

NEW ORLEANS SAINTS

Influenced by the rich culture and history of their hometown, the New Orleans Saints are held sacred to their fans.

WHO DAT?
SAINTS
DAT
D

"Who dat?" might be chanted from the stands, but the Saints have made their name known to everyone they have played.

KICK OFF

The Saints formed on November 1, 1966. They began to play in 1967. Like many new teams, the Saints struggled at first. Their struggles just lasted a bit longer than others.

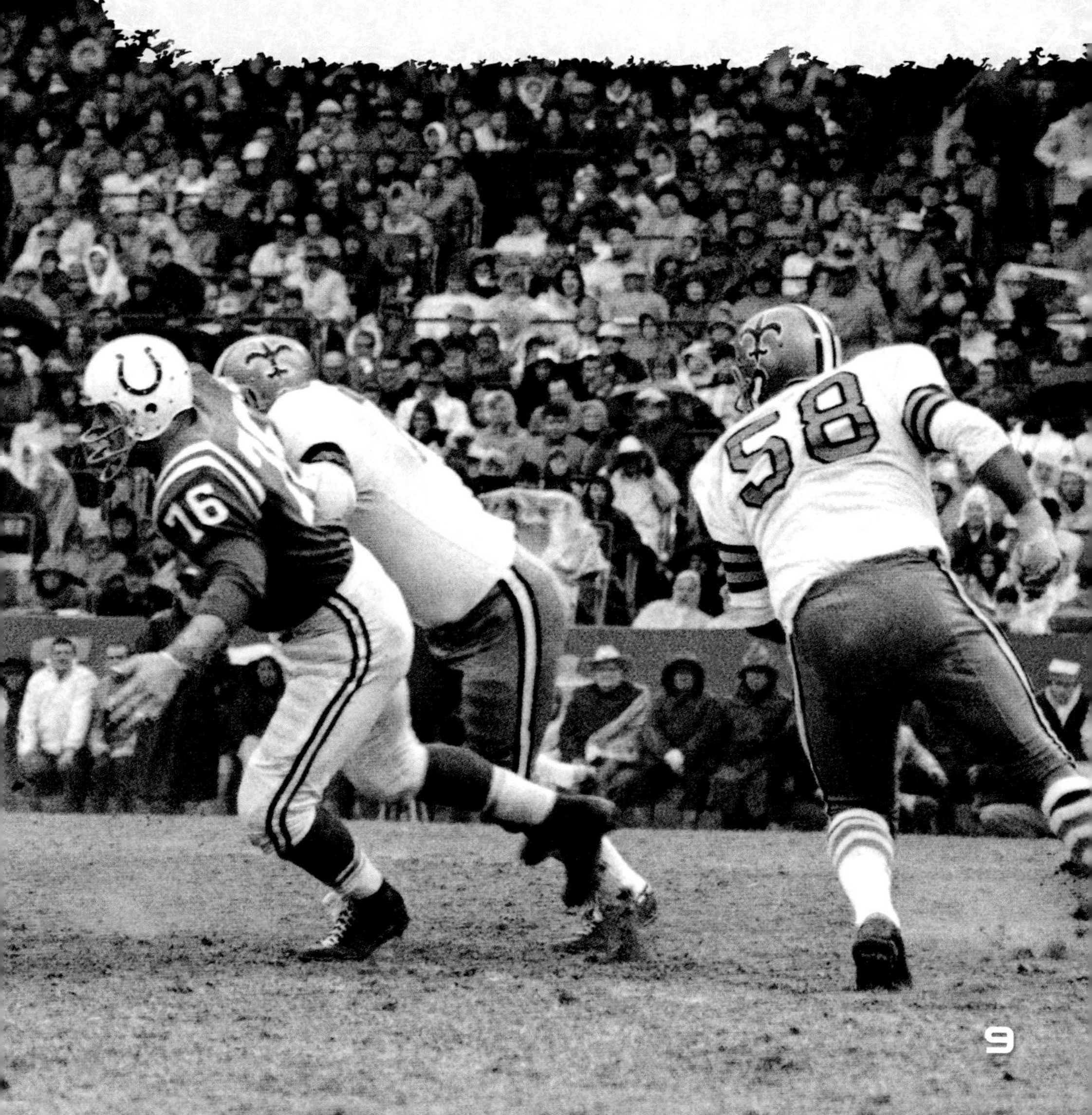

The Saints were nicknamed the
"Aints" because they did not
have a winning season for more
than 20 years.

The Saints began having some
success in the 1987 season, and
even made it to the playoffs!

Unfortunately, they lost to the Minnesota Vikings 44–10.

TEAM RECAPS

The Saints made it back to the playoffs in the 1990, 1991, and 1992 seasons. Sadly, they did not advance past the first playoff game in any of those years.

The Saints beat the Saint Louis Rams 31–28 at the 2000 playoffs. It was their first playoff win! In 2005, **Hurricane** Katrina devastated the city of New Orleans. The Saints played their home games in San Antonio, Texas, for the rest of the season.

The Saints worked hard during the 2009 season and made it to **Super Bowl** XLIV. They beat the Indianapolis Colts in their first Big Game appearance! After the destructive **hurricane** and other struggles, the Saints were able to bring a little happiness to their hometown.

The Saints won their divisional playoff game following the 2018 season. At the **NFC** Championship, a blown call had the Saints lose to the Rams 26–23 in **overtime**.

In 2020, the Saints got first place in their division for the 4th season in a row. They won the 2020 **Wild Card** Playoffs against the Bears. The Saints became the first team to sweep the **NFC** South division!

HALL OF
FAME
24

Linebacker Rickey Jackson played for the Saints for most of his career. He is the all-time leader for the team in tackles with 1,104, and 115 **sacks**. Jackson was **inducted** into the Pro Football Hall of Fame in 2010.

Marques Colston played for the Saints his entire career. He is the all-time career touchdown leader for the team with 72. He set Saints franchise records for most receptions with 711. As well as the most career receiving yards with 9,759. Colston was inducted into the **Saints Hall of Fame** in 2019.

During his first season in 2006, Drew Brees helped the Saints reach the **NFC** championship for the first time. In 2010, he led the team to win **Super Bowl** XLIV! When Brees retired in 2021, he had broken many team and NFL passing records in his 15 seasons with the Saints.

SAINTS
NFL
29

GLOSSARY

hurricane – a tropical storm with strong, circular winds, rain, thunder, and lightning.

National Football Conference (NFC) – one of two major conferences of the NFL. Each conference contains 16 teams split into four divisions. The winner of the NFC championship plays the AFC winner at the Super Bowl.

overtime – additional minutes added to a tied-up game giving each team a chance to win.

Saints Hall of Fame – founded in 1987, a museum that inducts one to two former players or coaches into its Hall of Fame every year based on their accomplishments with the team.

Super Bowl – the NFL championship game, played once a year.

Wild Card Round – the first round of the playoffs. Each of the two conferences send four division champions and three wild-card teams to its postseason.

ONLINE RESOURCES

Booklinks
NONFICTION NETWORK
FREE! ONLINE NONFICTION RESOURCES

To learn more about the New Orleans Saints, please visit **abdobooklinks.com** or scan this QR code. These links are routinely monitored and updated to provide the most current information available.